Still

In the Midst of
the Storm

Valerie Toles

HATCHBACK Publishing
Genesee, MI

Still Standing in the Midst of the Storm
©2017 Valerie Toles

Unless otherwise noted, Scripture take from the New King James Version Spirit-Filled Life Bible®. Copyright©1991 by Thomas Nelson, Inc. Used by permission. All rights reserved.

Published by
HATCHBACK Publishing
Genesee, Michigan 48437
Since 2005
www.hatchbackpublishing.com
The views, opinions and words expressed in this book are those of the author and do not necessarily reflect the position of HATCHBACK Publishing LLC or its owners

Cover Design by Ouan Ollie

ISBN 978-0-9988295-8-6

Printed in USA
10 9 8 7 6 5 4 3 2 1

For Worldwide Distribution

Dedication

First to my mother, the late Zola Stitt

Suicidal Survivors

This is also for the young girls who have been abused and to the survivors who have come out.

And to the late Nella Bates

Contents

Acknowledgements

I would like to give a heartfelt thanks to all the people who have been a support to me in this life's journey.

I would like to thank each person individually for the love, support and prayers they have provided for me in writing this book but the list would be larger than the book.

Special Thanks

My son, Michael Toles
My Family

Aunt Pat
Aunt Dorothy Strong
Mother Clara Callaway
Shiletta Murray
Margaret Jones
Lela Adams
Mary Davis
Deborah Wise
Johnnetta Knott
Cheryl Osborn
Deborah Miller
Pamela Y. Loving-Copeland
Sandy Mcwen

Jackie and Jamola Wilson
Calardine and Collion Stevens
Lupita Rippy
Eric Thomas, Entrepreneur

Pastor Charles Williams
Apostle Ruby Johnson
Pastor Clarence and First Lady Barbara Lewis
Bishop Ernest and Ann Turner
Pastor Melvin and Barbara Davis
Pastor Sherry Lyn Britton
Pastor Lonnie and Frances Brown

Verona Terry, Miss Dunn, Mary Bradshaw and
Flint Job Corps
Beverly Towns, Maxine McCormick and the
FWCC Intercessory Team

Most of all I want to acknowledge and thank
Mr. Donnie Younger

I give honor and thanks to the Most High God
who is the head of my life.

*I have planted, Apollos watered but God gives
the increase.* (I Corinthians 3:6)

God I thank You it is You who gives increase in
every area of our lives. Thank You for increasing
every area.

Special Words

I met Valerie thirty-four years ago and have personally known her twenty-four years. Over those years, I have watched her face many challenges but with those challenges has come growth. I have particularly seen her faith grow when she was fighting for her life and trusting God after she was diagnosed with breast cancer. She would quote scriptures and pray the Word of God. During those times, I joined her in prayer and encouraged her in her faith.

Earlier this year Valerie visited our church, Divine Grace Ministries. She had a knot on her hand and was advised she needed surgery. My husband, Apostle Bobby Johnson and I prayed for a creative miracle. The knot went away and she no longer needed surgery. Additionally, I watched her be delivered from some areas in her past that had left deep scars. Valerie is a fighter! With everything she's gone through in life, the cancer, chemo, radiation, heart problems, and fatigue, you would never know it looking at her.

When I found out the cancer had returned and spread to her liver, I became quite concerned. My husband and I would pray with and speak life over her. She had people praying for her all around the world. When she told me they wanted to cut the cancer out of her liver I was concerned the cancer would spread. Valerie called and let me speak with the doctor. She advised me Valerie was a rare case, felt the surgery would be successful, and the liver would regenerate itself.

So we believed God for another creative miracle. Since that time, Valerie gave me a praise report that the surgery was successful and her liver has already started regenerating itself!

I'm praying that purpose and destiny be fulfilled in her life.

Prophetess Mary Johnson

Foreword

I met Valerie over thirty-four years ago at Wallis Restaurant in Flint, Michigan. I went into the ladies' room and saw a young woman in her twenties crying. I asked her what was wrong and she started telling me her problems. She said she wanted to commit suicide. This really touched me because I had some of the same thoughts before.

Immediately I wanted to help her so I gave her my number. We started talking and I realized she needed a lot of support. That is what I began to do. I encouraged her. She started believing in herself and began to see what her life was worth.

I saw her mind starting to change. She began to better herself in her gifting and was motivated in her creative craft.

I have been in her life since our first meeting. God put Valerie in my heart. It makes me happy to see her go forward and do what she is called to do in the earth.

Ethel Oden

Introduction

Sometimes in life we have obstacles, hindrances and blockages in our way. They come to stop us and block us from doing what God desires us to do.

God has carried me when I did not know what to do. He saw the best in me. People did not see what God saw. They did not see my potential. In His tender mercy, He is taking the broken and scattered pieces of my life and making it into a beautiful masterpiece. In this process he has given me beauty for ashes.

I started taking chemo in 2014, some of the people I started off taking chemo with are not here today. I know of people who have had fourth stage cancer and have died. God has kept me for a reason. I am still standing in the midst of the storm.

For I know the thoughts that I think toward you, says the Lord, thoughts of peace and not of evil, to give you a future and a hope.

Jeremiah 29:14

To console those who mourn in Zion, To give them beauty for ashes,

The oil of joy for mourning,
The garment of praise for the spirit of heaviness

Isaiah 61: 3a

One of my friends was helping me to move out of my home into an apartment. I will never forget this day, December 30th. The enemy did not want me to make it out of that house - alive. We were working, moving things out of the attic and I fell through the dry wall on the attic floor. The attic collapsed under me - I was hanging onto the support beam. She couldn't help me and I couldn't help myself. I was holding on for my life.

She ran down the stairs and went outside calling for help. There happened to be garbage men who were coming by the house. They stopped their route, called their supervisor about the emergency and assisted me to safety. They also got the rest of my things from the attic. God sent them at just the right moment when I needed them.

The attacks have been severe on my life. God knows our greatness and His plans for us. He has an expected end that we cannot see. God has the blueprint of my life.

My husband June 2013. I was moving out of my house on December 30, 2013. That day I almost lost my life.

Once I was at a four-way stop intersection. I was moving forward and I saw the car coming. It was coming so fast, I could not get out of the way. I tried to speed up, after he hit me, my car flipped over twice. When it was over I was in the backseat and my car was totaled.

Another time I was behind a semi-truck. He began to back up and I could not back up fast enough. The whole front end of my car was smashed. I got out without a scratch. And yet, I am still standing…

Chapter 1

The Beginning

Celebrating Christmas and Easter proved to be the happiest times of my life, The gifts and family gatherings is what made Christmas special, while dressing up in new clothes is what I loved about Easter.

Like many others, I came from a home where there was a lot of chaos. Sometimes when the parents come from a dysfunctional home the children grow up in dysfunction. When the house is chaotic it effects everyone.

My dad came from a dysfunctional home. He left his home at an early age. My dad was a provider for the family but he did not know how to relate as a father and a husband. Apparently there was no emotional and inner healing, he grew up with all kinds of problems in life. I didn't have a good relationship with my dad but I got my personality from my father. He was outgoing and a people person. He was a fun person to be around. Sometimes they say when you have a personality like someone in your life it can be difficult to get along with them ...because you are alike.

I did not get to know my dad until the end of his life. When he got sick he called on me all of the time and I had the opportunity to spend a lot of time with him. I would bring him to my house and cook for him. He would lay on my couch. I was forming a relationship with him when I found out that I had cancer. He was in the midst of dying of cancer.

I got a call to come to the hospital. The doctors said he would not make it through the night. When I arrived at the hospital, my family was in the waiting with the doctor. Everyone was crying. I told my oldest brother, Ervin, my aunt, Pat, Sis, and Geraldine Harper to get in a circle around my dad and pray. Where there is unity there is strength. Before the end of the night all of his vitals started to elevate. My dad lived three months longer.

The devil does not want us to come together because there is power, strength and deliverance in unity. His strategy is to keep us divided and it is just what the devil likes...division.

I took my father's death very hard. I was just getting to know him and form a good relationship then he died. I felt like I wasn't finished with this process and I grieved for a long time.

My parents had six children. I was the fifth child. I experienced a lot of loneliness. I had bad nerves and stayed fearful. When my father and my mother would fight, my brothers would sometimes try to help my mother. There was a lot of chaos in my home.

My journey began when I was in kindergarten. My first teachers were Ms. Oliver and Ms. Maggie in the units on Holmes Street. They were two doors down away from my home. Ms. Maggie was and tough. She was really hard on me. Ms. Oliver was loving teacher.

My grandmother passed away while I was in the kindergarten. This was my mother's mother. My mother cried a lot and it really hurt me to see her cry like that. My great-grandmother, on my father's side made us dresses to wear to the funeral. I loved going to my great-grandmother's house. She made cookies, pies, cakes, and clothes.

I was violated sexually starting in the kindergarten. A person close to the family molested me when I was just a little girl. I was given candy and quarters to be quiet. Like other children, I did not talk about it because I was afraid. I felt shame and guilt.

When I went to school, I acted out. I acted like the class clown. This caused me to have a lot of challenges in school. I was just acting out because of what I had been through. Instead of talking about what happened, I had a mental block. It's not good to hold secrets because it keeps you in bondage. It is important to find someone who you can trust and talk to. I didn't talk but I needed someone to listen. It kept me in bondage mentally and emotionally.

People are affected by abuse in many different ways. I did not do drugs, alcohol or prostitute myself. One of the major ways I was affected was by talking to anyone who would listen. Most of the time it was the wrong people. There are many addictions. I ended up with a "talking" addiction. I didn't think before I talked. I just wanted to relieve my pain. If I had kept it all inside, I may have had a mental break.

I believe my mother knew the truth the whole time but I never told her. I think mothers have an instinct, a special discernment.

Everywhere I went, I seemed to be abused verbally, emotionally and mentally some type of way. I had problems when I acted out in school. I had problems in some of my relationships. I had problems on my job.

When I was in middle school, I was not popular. I loved to go to the counselor's office. This gave me another reason to get out of the class. I was rebellious, disobedient, and angry.

I got saved at twelve years old. It was the first time I felt God. I was at a tent revival held by Bishop Raymond Dunlap. I didn't understand the Bible, and I ended up backsliding. It's better not to have a relationship with the Lord than having one and turning your back on Him. It's like turning your back on someone you really love.

I was kicked out of school in the eighth grade and ended up going to school for troubled kids and Street Academy which was an adult high school. They would pay us fifteen dollars a week to go to school. I started having suicidal thoughts.

When I was sixteen years old, I fell in love with a guy who was abusive. Years later he did apologize. Sometimes, in life, we can attract people that can be abusive and have unhealthy relationships if we are not healed.

The first person I told about being abused was my Godmother, Nellie Bates. I was sixteen years old. The school ended up sending me to see a therapist because my nerves were so bad.

When I went back to Northwestern High school, there was an abuse I dealt with there from a teacher. The teacher put me in front of the class so the other students could mock and torture me. I ran out of the class crying. At the end of my time there, I only needed two classes and work study. After that, I graduated.

I believe the spirit of rejection came in when I was a child. Rejection comes in many forms. It can come from the womb or the environment. My Godmother, Thelma Burkette, took to me as a little child, she could see some of the things I was going through. She took me as her own.

I applied for a job at General Motors and took a physical. After that they had a big layoff for years and I never got called back. I ended up working at a hospital. While working there, I was going to work, church and the clubs. Some of the people there didn't like me and some of the supervisors gave me a hard time. People I was close to were told to stay away from me and not to be my friend. I did not want them to get in trouble for talking to me. I felt like I was in a prison where I got to go home when the shift ended but I had to come back to prison the next day – that was the only difference.

Some of the people there disliked me but I did not want to lose my job. I was called names and felt tormented. They labeled me. People will apply labels to you that are not true.

No weapons formed against you shall prosper, and every tongue which rises against you in judgement You shall condemn.
Isaiah 54:17a

Even on my job weapons were formed but it did not prosper.

What then shall we say to these things? If God is for us, who can be against us?

Romans 8:31

It was painful for me to go to work, but God kept me in the midst of the storm. I thank God for keeping me and being there for me even though my back was against the wall. Sometimes my mouth got me into trouble because I tried to fight my own battle. Be careful what comes out of your mouth.

You are snared by the words of your mouth;
You are taken by the words of your mouth.

Proverbs 6:2

I was in a battle but it was not mine, it was the Lord's. We have to learn to take things to the Lord and not take them into our own hands. I got into a deeper hole with my mouth. Only God can get me out of this battle. Sometimes we have to be still and know that He is God and He will fight our battles. I was in the fire but I got out.

At the age of nineteen, my nerves were so bad because of all of the abuse I went through. I was put on nerve pills because of the abuse. I would itch a lot and my body broke out in hives. I had a lot of trouble on the job and I had some unhealthy relationships. I felt like I had nothing to live for. The suicidal thoughts continued.

I stayed on sick leave a lot to get away from the torture. Once when I went on sick leave, one of the co-workers told me what was on my sick leave papers. I felt betrayed because they were sharing my personal, confidential information with others.

Working on this job and dealing with all of this drove me back to God. I told God I would really get saved to keep my job. Sometimes I even felt like I couldn't hold my head up but I learned God is the glory and the lifter of my head.

LORD, how they have increased who trouble me! Many are they who rise up against me. Many are they who say of me, "There is no help for him in God." Selah

But You, O LORD, are a shield for me, My glory and the One who lifts my head.

Psalm 3:1-3

Chapter 2

Called Into Ministry

While at work, instead of going to lunch, I would go into the Ladies lounge. I would fast, pray and read my Bible. Sometimes I would walk into the rooms of the sick patients and pray. As a teenage girl, at the age of sixteen, I did volunteer work at the hospital as a Candy Striper. When I got older I did pastoral care in the hospital. I would go from room to room praying for the sick.

See, all those labels did not fit me because I was a woman who loved God and His Word. I was a giver and there was work for me to do. The enemy used people to try to destroy my name and my character.

> *A good name is to be chosen rather than great riches, loving favor rather than silver and gold.*

Proverbs 22:1

I was always speaking the Word of God to people, witnessing to them and bringing many people to church in my car. It was more of a lifestyle to me. I did not know what it was called.

I was with Victory Miracle Temple. We would fast three days in the church and then go out on the street with drug addicts. Sometimes we don't fit in all groups. God put me in the right group. He used me to bring in the souls. I saw a man out in the streets, he was on heavy drugs. I prayed for him, and took him to church. This man got healed and delivered. He would testify about it.

There was this one young lady I met, who was high on drugs. I took her to church and she was prayed back to sobriety. She later went to college and got her degree.

I found out later I had a call to evangelism with a prophetic gift. There was one woman who God used me to pray for on the job. We were working across from each other on the line. She said she had a headache. I prayed for her and later she told me she was instantly healed from her headache.

One day I was doing my job, not bothering anybody. A supervisor came up, started harassing me and said she was going to get me fired. I kept right on praying like she wasn't there. Five minutes later this particular supervisor passed out.

I went to the hospitals and the nursing homes praying and winning souls to Christ.

I stayed under attack on my job. Sometimes before my job even started, I was in trouble. One day God spoke to me and said to look up and write out all of the scriptures on strength. I told my mother God was preparing me for something. I knew something was coming but I did not know what it was. I got written up and terminated after ten years of being on the job. I had just bought a new car. I didn't know how I was going to pay for it but I had a peace like I never had before in my life. My car insurance got paid up for two years through unemployment and the help of a community agency. God touched someone's heart and my car got paid off. People thought I worked in General Motors. God touched people and I was blessed because of it. In the end, I got a better paying job.

I paid my tithes and God rebuked the devour, just as the scripture says he will do. He is a Way-Maker. I always pay my tithes. I am a believer and a tithes-payer. I've seen God make a way too many times not to be either. I know Him to be a doctor in the sick room, a provider and a lawyer in the court room!

For I know the thoughts that I think toward you, says the Lord, thoughts of peace and not of evil, to give you a future and a hope.

Jeremiah 29:11

Thus says the LORD, who makes a way in the sea and a path through the mighty waters,

Isaiah 43:16

When you pass through the waters, I will be with you; And through the rivers, they shall not overflow you. When you walk through the fire you shall not be burned. Nor shall the flame scorch you.

Isaiah 43:2

I was in the fire, I didn't get burned and I came out without a scratch.

Chapter 3

My Marraige

In 1996, my brother died of cancer. My fiancé and I had already made plans to get married. I got married a day before my brother's funeral. I didn't have a wedding, but I had a huge reception.

I lived in a nice home. My husband was an excellent provider. When I met my husband he had a painting company. He was making enough to survive. He began thriving and got huge jobs in our area. He painted a lot of churches, Hurley Clinics, doctor's offices, Sylvester Broome Center, Bishop Airport, University of Michigan and Carmen-Ainsworth High School to name a few.

The first eight years of my marriage was absolutely wonderful. But when you lose communication there is no marriage. It is best to get to know a person before you get married, putting everything on the table and be honest. After eight and a half years of marriage, the communication was gone. You can be married and lonely. Sometimes in life, people do not know what you've gone through. I found out later my husband went through some storms and tough times in his life. He had been incarcerated, when he was younger. But no matter what you go through, God can turn your life around. He can make you the head and not the tail. My husband had a good, thriving business. What God did for others He will do for you. Life is not beyond repair. God can make the wrong, right. He gave my husband a prosperous business. No matter what you have done in your life, God can turn your life around for the better, just like He did for me and my husband.

My husband grew up in the church and had a call of destiny on his life. Sometimes we don't get a chance to fulfill it. His father was a pastor, his mother, a mighty woman of God, was a missionary. My husband saw a lot growing up in the church as a pastor's son. He was discouraged about some things and eventually went a different way.

Then he got sick, it started with prostate cancer. He worked all of the time and didn't take care of himself like he should have. He had damage to his liver and eventually, he had a liver transplant. When I went to see him, it looked like he had every tube in him in the world. It seemed like they kept taking him to surgery. He had issues with bleeding. Through continued prayers the bleeding stopped. For a time he was unresponsive, I kept praying. Eventually he started moving his legs, then he opened his eyes. He woke up out of it and had the opportunity to spend the day with his son. God gave him a miracle to come through the transplant and come home.

I thank God for all of the prayers of the saints and the grace of God that brought him through the surgeries. He got to spend time with his family before he transitioned. We were still legally married and living in the same home at the time of his death, but we were estranged. You can live in the same house but not be together. Now I was a widow.

Chapter 4

Chosen By God

When you are chosen by God, you will be picked out to be picked on. A person can only take so much and then they will begin to act out because they don't understand. People judged me but they did not know me. Who wants to have a label put on them?

> *You know my reproach, my shame and my dishonor; my adversaries are all before You.*

Psalm 69:19

The devil put things out on me, by this I mean that people made accusations about me. People only know what they have heard. When you are chosen you can be perceived as different and peculiar. Some people don't understand you, they have a tendency to labels you. They don't know the things you have been through and it can cause misunderstandings. I feel that I have been misunderstood all of my life.

I don't even know the majority of the people who have said negative things about me. I believe it was the works of the enemy. When a person has a call of destiny and purpose, the devil will try to destroy you.

The thief comes only the kill, steal, and destroy. I have come that you might have life and have it more abundantly. John 10:10

For this purpose the Son of God was manifested, that he might destroy the devil. I John 3:9

God puts gifts on the inside of you. You cannot see what other people see. You have to have spiritual eyes to see. Sometimes people can see things about you. Sometimes people will try to block, stop and hinder you from fulfilling your destiny and purpose. They will speak evil against you and say things which are not true. Even though they have a spiritual eye, gifts and callings are without repentance.

God will cancel every assignment of word curses and evil wishes against you. I had to ask God to clear my name from the haters. God is greater than the devil and the haters. We have the Greater One living on the inside of us.

God is our defense. He will uphold us and He is the Lord God that will help us. He is more than the whole world against us. The battle is not ours but the Lord's.

What then shall we say to these things? If God is for us, who can be against us?

Romans 8:31

We can pray and feel like God is not there. We can sometimes find ourselves in the pit. This is the pit of depression, hurt, loneliness, sorrow or whatever. If we just wait, He will bring us out. Sometimes we pray and believe God but we have to wait on the answer. Sometimes the answer does not come immediately. While we are waiting, we praise Him in the midst of every storm.

But those who wait on the LORD shall renew their strength; they shall mount up with wings like eagles, they shall run and not be weary, they shall walk and not faint.

Isaiah 40:31

There was a man of God who spoke over my life and said to me, "God is going to put you on display." It is important to activate, cultivate and stir up the gift on the inside. God will move things and people will walk out of your life. There are times and seasons you must spend alone with God.

It seemed as though I did not fit in. Several times I have been misunderstood, betrayed, lied on, backstabbed, and persecuted. But God! I am still standing! Still standing with my hands lifted up and my heart filled with praise.

Lord, how they have increased who trouble me! Many are they who rise up against me. Many are they who say of me, "There is no help for him in God." But You, O Lord, are a shield for me, My glory and the One who lifts my head.

Psalm 3:1-3

I don't have to hold my head down any more.

Church Hurt

I went to church and I did not fit in. People called it "church hopping." The truth was, I was really just looking to fit in…somewhere.

I went to one church and I felt at home…for a while. I have left several times. The pastor said to me, "I don't care where you run off to, you are still my daughter. I don't care where you go."

Even when we are in church, our faith is tried and tested. Sometimes God can put us in a hard place and we run from that. We may be put in a place to endure and not to run off. While in these places we think it is the devil and it is really God – like when we are overlooked and not used in ministry. I did, however, have opportunities occasionally to lead the prayer and speak in several churches that I attended.

A lot of churches have cliques and their favorites. Sometimes the most gifted people are the ones left sitting in the pews. I was not always used in ministry which led me to feel like I did not fit. Many times when I did go to church, I saw things that made me feel worse than when I came. But not every church is the same. That's why we have to keep our eyes on Jesus and not people.

Innocent people come looking for help in some of these places and they are taken advantage of. Sometimes, some of these people are the most gifted.

They find themselves in situations where they are getting used and taken for their money. Some of these leaders and people hide behind the Name of Jesus and they are not of God. But God said He will give us shepherds after his own heart. A real father will care and watch out for his children.

And I will give you shepherds according to My heart, who will feed you with knowledge and understanding.

Jeremiah 3:15

Beloved, do not believe every spirit, but test the spirits, whether they are of God; because many false prophets have gone out into the world.

John 4:1

We have to be able to discern whether the spirit is of God or not. God will unplug our ears and remove the veil, the scales from our eyes so we can see. He gave us seeing eyes and hearing ears to see into the spirit realm.

Some people are spiritually blind so they are deceived and follow deception. They will be at a church because they say, "My grand-mama, my daddy and my mama went there, so this is where I am going to stay." Sometimes in these places God will show us some things, but we do not want to see.

At times people come to church and they are so hurt. They are very sensitive and easily offended, but they are looking for help. We must learn how to walk in love with each other.

When we are obedient to God we are in a place of safety and this is where miracles happen.

When the waste places have been broken down and stomped on, God will rebuild that which is torn down. Sometimes people are so quick to throw away people. We have to watch what we are willing to throw away.

Watch who you reject and who you stomp on. You might have to call that very same person to pray for you or give you a cup of water. You do not know where God is taking a person in their life.

Rejection

Sometimes people will reject you for many reasons. Whatever the cause, it is painful. Rejection was something I was familiar with and had dealt with for a long time.

You can try to do things for people and they want to take advantage of you. They try to take you for a ride and take your kindness for weakness. People who I thought were friends turned their back and walked away. I have been denied invitations to parties and dinners. Sometimes you think you have a friend and you don't. This type of betrayal hurts.

Jesus was despised and rejected by men. Just as Jesus suffered rejection so may we too be rejected. Jesus was betrayed, went through grief and sorrow, so will we. Jesus feels our pain.

Isaiah 53:3 says:
A man of sorrows and acquainted with grief.

At these times I meditated on the following scripture:

The Lord has appeared of old to me saying:
"Yes, I have loved you with an everlasting love;
therefore with lovingkindness I have drawn you."

Jeremiah 31:3

I have been lied on, turned on and falsely accused. I have been in the storm of hatred, betrayal and persecution. I've dealt with imprisonment in my mind. .I have had mountains of rejection, unforgiveness, sorrow, pain, and family dysfunction.

But there is a scripture which always caused me to believe again:

*I will offer to You the sacrifice of thanksgiving,
and I will call upon the
name of the Lord*

Psalm 116:17

And...I am still standing.

Losses

People experience loss in life and I was included. Sometimes it is not just the loss from a death. It can be the loss of a job, money, friends and relationships.

You can also experience a loss if your child is in jail or prison. You can also lose them to drugs, alcohol or the streets. When a child begins to show rebellion, which happens before the loss, most of the time this is due to them having pain on the inside.

I was a disobedient and rebellious child. We live in a land where disobedient and rebellious children are running rampant. One time I was talking back to my mother and when I went outside, I was met with trouble.

My son and I went through some storms when his father became very ill and passed away. They had a very close relationship and when his father died, I believe this caused him to become rebellious, angry and disobedient. I also believe it caused him

42

to make wrong choices for his life. Now there are consequences for every choice we make whether good or bad, but we know God gives everybody a chance to get it right. I continue to daily pray for my son.

For parents who are dealing with angry and rebellious children, just remember God gives everyone another chance to get it right. I want you to know whatever you go through God is in the midst. He is a refuge and strength, a very present help in time of trouble.

Joy

On the other side of rejection and loss is joy. I find joy getting up in the morning and putting beautiful things together. God gave me a gift to beautify.

I find joy in witnessing. I don't meet any strangers. I find joy in praying for the sick, helping people and giving.

I love waking up and seeing the sun, traveling to different places, and just being alive. I thank God for life!

I find joy in the Word of God. I've seen it work over and over again.

"...Do not sorrow, for the joy of the Lord is your strength."

Nehemiah 8:10b

Chapter 5

Medical Reports

As soon as something is wrong and you go to the doctor, the first thing they want to say is cancer. Fear comes to you immediately. *Am I going to make it through this?*

But the Lord speaks, "Fear not, I am with thee!"

We have to learn to speak life consistently over ourselves. Faith is believing our God for the impossible. Speak life whenever someone wants to speak death or when you see it.

"But I will deliver you in that day," says the Lord, "and you shall not be given into the hand of the men of whom you are afraid. For I will surely deliver you, and you shall not fall by the sword; but your life shall be as a prize to you, because you have put your trust in Me," says the Lord.'"

Jeremiah 39: 17-18

The Lord is my strength and my song. I shall not die, but live, and declare the works of the Lord.

Psalm 118: 14, 17

Cancer...Three Times

One day I felt my breast leaking. It was blood. My dad lay dying of bone cancer when I got my first diagnosis in 2002 of breast cancer.

The second week of chemotherapy, I woke up in the morning and my hair was in the bed. I had to have my hair shaved off. I called it the "Red Devil Chemo." Eventually, all of my hair grew back.

Out of this experience, I founded the Faith, Hope and Love Organization.

Statements

Aasiyah Aquil
Medical Assistant of Dr. Rizwan Danish
Speaker at Faith, Love, and Hope Support Group

When Valerie first came, she was terrified. She had lots of questions. She wanted it fixed and she wanted it fixed now. These are all normal reactions.

Valerie talked about her faith a lot. Having faith is important.

Once she really accepted what was happening, she reached out to others, talking to them about her journey. She also asked others about their journey.

Valerie went to support groups but culturally, she wanted something different. She felt as though the needs of the people were not being met. She aggressively went to work to get who and what she needed to start her own support group and to get the job done. This became more than just something to do for Valerie, more than a job. She was in tune with the people.

Valerie is a person who is hard to forget. She is often misunderstood but you have to take the time to just listen to her. It is often too easy to judge a book by its cover.

Linda Weisenberger RN
Genesys/Hurley Cancer Institute
Chemotherapy Nurse

When Valerie first came in she was in high stress, strong and excitable but she was also detailed-oriented. She asked lots of questions and wanted to know exactly what was going on with her treatment.

In November 2002, Valerie started six cycles of chemotherapy every three weeks. She was finished in February 2003. She was given three different types of chemo.

Some of the side effects from this cycle were: hair loss, extreme fatigue, nausea, diarrhea, aches, and pains. Her tongue, nails and feet turned black.

She was later diagnosed with stage two multifocal invasive ductal carcinoma.

Dr. Raouf Mikhail, MD
Chief of Surgery at Hurley Medical Center
Hurley Cancer Center Director
Speaker at Faith, Hope and Love Support Group

Valarie took cancer as a mission for fighting breast cancer. She started a support group at the Sylvester Broome Center. This support group attracted a lot of people, well over a hundred. She had speakers, donations, musicians and preachers. I thought it was great for her to be an advocate.

The people were saying they didn't find help in any other support groups that were available at this time. Valerie had what was needed. She had connections. She is a very special person. She did all of this and it was nothing about it for herself, instead it was for others.

In the last twenty years treatment has improved. The treatment and approach in the last five years which did not exist has given hope when people then were in hopeless situations.

Margaret Murray-Wright, MSN, RN
Administrator of Oncology Services
Associate Director of Undergraduate Nursing

Programs
Clinical Assistant Professor

One patient had shared how the support group was boring. We got together a good team of people and Valerie was the driving board. She has always been a supporter of cancer survivors. She would push the boundaries to make sure people were healthy. She would even make sure we tackled the uncomfortable issues. She was very effective in getting the message out.

Some people who showed up to the support group came angry because they had cancer. Valerie made sure people had faith, education and food.

Valarie was a great leader of the Faith, Hope, and Love Support Group.

Danita Roberts
Cancer Center Coordinator

Valerie has a heart to reach out to people. She helped coordinate the support group. She had the flyers, the programs and the refreshments. She took care of the logistics and there was very good attendance.

The room was filled with cancer patients, survivors, their family members, and caregivers. It was well supported and needed in the community. She had speakers, music, prayer, testimonies and a variety of other components.

***

The side effects of some of the medicine and chemotherapy is it can leave a bitter taste in your mouth which makes you feel self-conscious. I was weak and fatigued. I was cancer free for eleven years.

One day my toe started hurting so I went to the foot doctor. He asked me how long had that black spot been on my foot. I told him I did not know because I was not aware it was there.

They drilled a hole in the spot and sent some of it to Ann Arbor. It came back as cancer. Another test was taken, it came back non-cancerous.

A couple of months later, my side started hurting. Someone kept telling me I better go and have it checked out. The next day after I did, they told me I had a huge mass.

You have to make sure you ask God to connect you to the right doctor. As long as I can fulfill destiny and purpose, I am satisfied.

Dr. Caroline Matthews, M.D.

The liver mass was diagnosed in October 2014. At this time it was eighteen centimeters. This was metastasized from the breast cancer. In metastasis, cancer cells break away from where they first formed, travel through the blood or lymph system and form new tumors in other parts of the body.

The prognosis ten years ago was very poor. There are many different medications and treatment options now. All of these things are new within the last years.

Dr. Madan Arora, MD
Karmanos Cancer Institute

On seeing Valerie, we immediately put her on Neulasta. This medicine is long lasting and it helps to keep the white blood cell count up. Some of the side effects to this medicine are headaches and often tired. We also prescribed pain pills.

We gave her chemo two weeks straight then she came in for the shot. Valerie was in the beginning of early stage in 2002. We treated her then with an intention to cure. It was treatable but we did more to control it.

Valerie has a positive spirit. She is a fighter with a good attitude. She has a good support system. I know because she is always on the phone. When you have support it is much more helpful. You find yourself in better shape.

The mass started at eighteen centimeters in October 2014 and as of June 2016, it is now 6.6 by 7.8.

Penny
Chemo Nurse at Karmanos Cancer Institute

Whenever Valerie walked in she was always beautiful. She would inspire others to look good and to feel good. She meets no strangers and makes lots of friends. She should start the support group again.

Kathy
Chemo Nurse at Karmanos Cancer Institute

Valerie is a lovely woman with strong faith. She loves to share her faith and pray with others. She has an uplifting personality, always looks good and is well dressed.

Valerie cheers people up when she walks in. It's like sunshine walking into a room. Being uplifting, hopeful and having the spirituality to share with others makes Valerie the person we like to have around.

Jean Battles, LMSW
Karmanos Cancer Institute

Valerie is definitely a survivor. "I can't" is not a part of her vocabulary. I often tell Valerie of my admiration of her determination to move forward with her life. Bit by bit she has learned to trust her instincts as to where she needs to focus her energy. Life may not have been the most kind to her in the beginning but she has persevered and risen above the angst that was forced upon her in her younger years.

Valerie is community conscious and very generous. She carries a lot of love in her heart and finds many ways to touch others and try to make a difference in their lives.

I told Dr. Danish I was writing a book. I also went to see him because I wanted his opinion on what I should do with the latest development I was facing.

Dr. Rizwan Danish – Oncologist
Hurley Medical Center

The type of energy Valerie has makes things happen. She wears her emotions on her sleeve but she is upbeat and bubbly. Valerie is such a positive person that when she got the news in 2002 that she had breast cancer, it was hard for her to believe. That is a normal reaction though. It takes a minute to wrap your head around it.

When you start talking about things like surgery, treatment, and chemo, all of this information is overwhelming. I offered her the most aggressive treatment and she said yes.

When a young woman loses her breast, it attacks her femininity, what she feels about herself and how others see her. Privately, it can also affect her relationships. In spite of it all, Valerie was interested in living.

We put her on Tamoxifen. The side effects are hot flashes, moodiness and weight gain.

There is a genetic testing which we can see where several genes run in a family and it makes them predisposed to cancer. We can see if a person has a certain gene where they are eighty-five percent predisposed to breast cancer and sixty to sixty-five percent predisposed to ovarian cancer. It checks for changes in the genes called BRCA1 and BRCA 2.

**

I asked Dr. Danish if it was his family member facing different types of cancer, where would he send them. He gave me his opinion.

If it was my family, if they had Melanoma, I would send them to Ann Arbor, Michigan. If it was a brain meningioma, I would send them to California. If it was primary breast cancer, I would send them to Hurley Hospital in Flint.

As an Oncologist, we deal with medical, surgical and radiation. I would always suggest a person to get a highly qualified second opinion.

After further conversation he asked, "Valerie, you don't have liver cancer do you?" He had tears in his eyes. He gave me a hug and his suggestion was for me to go to Henry Ford Hospital. At that time, he had no idea I was already scheduled for surgery in Ann Arbor.

I canceled that surgery and went to Henry Ford Hospital. Before I went to Henry Ford Hospital, the plan was for me to be on chemo for the rest of my life and they were just going to try and make me comfortable. It was the best move I ever made.

Dr. Sandeep Grewal M.D.
Clinical Assistant Professor of Medicine
Medical Oncology and Hematology

Dr. Grewal: "We are waiting to see if your liver is growing back properly. Are you nervous?"

Me: "No. Prayer brought me through this far and people are praying for me."

Dr. Grewal: "This is unusual because the type of medicine we normally give for this is bad for the heart but because of your side effects we stopped giving them to you. At the time of your surgery, your mass was 10.5 centimeters. We do not expect to see anything on your scan, this is remarkable. If we see nothing then your cancer is in remission but there is no cure."

Me: "I curse that in the Name of Jesus. When I feel a peace then I know I'm alright."

The next morning I was scheduled to be at Henry Ford Hospital for a follow-up visit.

Dr. Kelly M Collins, MD
Transplant and Hepatobiliary Surgery

When Valerie came to us, we knew it was going to be a process from six to eight months. First she had to have the Yttrium-90 Radio embolization which is done by an interventional radiologist. This procedure are beads which carry the radiation to the tumor. This had a two-fold purpose for us. It

55

shrinks the tumor and it gives us time to observe her and the liver tissue.

When we further observed Valerie, we saw the mass contained on one spot in the liver. We planned to take the tumor out surgically. This was a unique procedure. Without the Y-90 procedure, we would not have been able to take the tumor out.

In my opinion, Valerie is very intense and has a passion for learning. She is accepting, open and willing to follow our advice with the help of her supportive community. She is one tough cookie.

***

People were asking me what stage cancer was this and I would tell them I did not know, because I didn't. The doctor didn't tell me. I found out from another doctor it was stage four.

There are resources for paying for chemotherapy. The social worker is the person to talk to. I have had five grants to help me pay for mine.

People always need to go for a second opinion.

It's been pain and hell a lot of my days. I don't look like what I've been through. God has put my life on display for His glory. And He alone helped me and I am still standing in the midst of the storm!

Forgiveness is the Key

When we clean our homes we get rid of clutter and we feel renewed and have a new sense of purpose. In the spiritual world, getting rid of clutter is like cleaning your spiritual home, getting rid of pain and hurt. We do this by forgiving others. When we refuse to forgive others, it hurts our soul and keeps us from moving forward.

Hebrews 12.1

Wherefore seeing we are also compassed about with so great a cloud of witnesses, let us lay aside every weight and sin that does so easily beset us. And let us run with patience the race that is before us.

When you run in a race you run to win. This means the weight must come of -we must be at our best. We cannot do this with unforgiveness and sin in our hearts. If we have things we have held onto for years, we need to ask God to help us let them go.

Psalms 51.10

Create in me a clean heart oh God, and renew a right spirit within me.

We need to ask God to heal our minds of all glut and rubble. Ask God for healthy thinking and a new mindset. When our minds are full of clutter, we cannot think straight. We should ask for a clarity of thought, clarity of vision, and clarity of purpose.

For speaking engagements, please contact
Valerie Toles (810) 293-5350

Troubled marriages

Scriptures of Forgiveness and the Importance of Forgiveness.

Work sheet about Forgiveness.

Not easy to Forgive.

49021757R00033

Made in the USA
Columbia, SC
18 January 2019